Hunting
TURKEYS

Hines Lambert

PowerKiDS press.

New York

Published in 2013 by The Rosen Publishing Group, Inc.
29 East 21st Street, New York, NY 10010

First Edition

Editor: Amelie von Zumbusch
Book Design: Kate Laczynski

Photo Credits: Background graphic © iStockphoto.com/Andrea Zanchi; sidebar binoculars © iStockphoto.com, Feng Yu; cover Royce Bair/Flickr/Getty Images; p. 5 Jeff Banke/Shutterstock.com; p. 6 © iStockphoto.com/Pau Tessier; p. 7 Elizabeth Root Blackmer/Flickr/Getty Images; p. 8 Tim Laman/National Geographic/Getty Image pp. 9, 22, 29 iStockphoto/Thinkstock; pp. 10, 12 Dewayne Flowers/Shutterstock.com; p. 11 Mag. Alban Egger/Shutterstock.com; p. 13 (left) Sharon Day/Shutterstock.com; p. 13 (right) James Zipp/Photo Researchers Getty Images; p. 15 Stephanie Frey/Shutterstock.com; pp. 16, 17 Wichita Eagle/McClatchy-Tribune/Getty Images; p. 18 David Watkins/Shutterstock.com; p. 19 (top) John Carey/Photolibrary/Getty Images; p. 19 (bottom) Ron Chapple Studios/Thinkstock; pp. 20, 23 (right), 26 Hemera/Thinkstock; p. 21 Miami Herald/ McClatchy-Tribune/Getty Images; p. 23 (left) Dave King/Dorling Kindersley/Getty Images; p. 24 Racheal Moore/Shutterstock.com; p. 25 Steve Oehlenschlager/Shutterstock.com; p. 27 © iStockphoto.com/Michael Olson; p. 28 © iStockphoto.com/Jon Huelskamp.

Library of Congress Cataloging-in-Publication Data

Lambert, Hines.
  Hunting turkeys / by Hines Lambert. — 1st ed.
     p. cm. — (Let's go hunting)
  Includes index.
  ISBN 978-1-4488-9660-8 (library binding) — ISBN 978-1-4488-9778-0 (pbk.) —
  ISBN 978-1-4488-9779-7 (6-pack)
  1. Turkey hunting—Juvenile literature. I. Title.
  SK325.T8L356 2013
  799.2'4645—dc23
                        2012023934

Manufactured in the United States of America

CPSIA Compliance Information: Batch #W13PK2: For Further Information contact Rosen Publishing, New York, New York at 1-800-237-9932

CONTENTS

Move Over, Bald Eagle 4

A Native Bird 6

Seasons and Bag Limits 8

Getting Ready 10

Finding the Turkey 12

Calls 14

Decoys 16

Shotguns 18

Know Your Target 20

Load That Muzzle 22

Bend That Bow 24

Any Day Can Be Thanksgiving 26

How Hunters Saved the Day 28

Hunting Tips 30

Glossary 31

Index 32

Websites 32

How many birds have their own holiday? Every Thanksgiving, millions of Americans feast on turkey. Thanksgiving is the most important holiday for many Americans, and the turkey is one of America's most important **game birds**. The wild turkey was very important to early American hunters. It often saved them from starving. Benjamin Franklin even wanted the turkey to be our national bird instead of the bald eagle!

Turkeys have lived in the United States for longer than most of the animals that Americans regularly eat. Unfortunately, Americans did not always value them. Wild turkeys nearly died out. Turkey hunters helped save them!

Do you enjoy eating turkey? If so, you might enjoy eating a turkey you hunted even more. Many turkey hunters prefer the taste of turkeys they have killed themselves.

This proud hunter has killed several turkeys. Turkey hunting is a sport with a long history in North America.

Turkeys have lived in North America for thousands of years. Today, there are five **subspecies** of North American turkeys. The most common is the eastern wild turkey, found in the eastern United States.

Male turkeys are called gobblers. You can recognize gobblers by the spurs on their legs. These look like long toenails. Gobblers also have beards, which are a group of feathers sticking out from their chests.

Each turkey has about 5,000 feathers.

During breeding season, turkeys will try to attack other turkeys. Turkeys challenge each other to be in charge of the flock.

Turkeys might look slow, but they can actually run as fast as 25 miles per hour (40 km/h). They can fly as fast as 55 miles per hour (89 km/h)! Turkeys prefer to be in the open when they eat and mate, but they like to hide in trees. An open field next to a forest is a good place to find turkeys.

Did You Know?

You can tell gobblers from females because they have larger, fanlike tails, brightly colored beards, and spurs. They also make a unique gobble that can be heard up to 1 mile (2 km) away!

Most states allow turkey hunting in the spring and the fall. Since turkeys mate in the spring, most states permit only gobbler hunting in the spring. Female turkeys, or hens, are laying eggs and raising chicks during this season. Many states allow hunters to shoot both gobblers and hens in the fall. The spring is a good time for hunting gobblers because they are on the move in search of hens. The fall is also a good time to hunt because it is when turkeys flock together.

Hens, such as this one, can generally be hunted only in the fall.

Gobblers are also known as toms. They can be hunted in either the spring or the fall.

You must get a hunting **license** before you can hunt turkeys. Your state's website will have information about how to get your license. Most states allow you to shoot a certain number of turkeys. This is called the **bag limit**. Always make sure you know your state's bag limit!

Did You Know?

Female turkeys care for their young on their own for a few days, but then the young turkeys join their mothers in large hen and chick flocks.

This turkey hunter's camouflage face mask, hat, and jacket will make it hard for a turkey to spot him.

It helps to find your hunting spot before the season begins. Look for an open field with trees nearby. Wild turkeys love open areas. They eat grasses, berries, and insects. If you find those, you have found a good spot.

Many of the best hunters like to hunt early in the morning. This is when gobblers leave their **roosts**, or the trees they sleep in, and start moving around. These hunters like to be in their spots before the Sun comes up.

Unlike many animals, turkeys can see colors well. Wearing **camouflage** is a must. Pick out a camouflage that matches your area. Turkeys are often scared away by hunters' faces. It is a good idea to wear a camouflage face mask.

These hunters are setting out on an early-morning turkey hunt.

You can find a turkey's roost by knowing what to look for. Most turkeys prefer trees with wide branches. It helps if the tree is near water. Turkeys make noise when they roost. Good turkey hunters must have sharp ears as well as eyes. It can be hard to see turkeys in their natural **habitat**. Hunters are not the only ones with camouflage!

A good turkey hunter is always on the lookout for turkeys.

Turkey tracks may look slightly different depending on whether they were made in sand, mud, or snow.

Wild turkeys spend most of the day on the ground. However, they do roost in trees for the night.

How do you know if your spot is near a good field? Look for turkey tracks. These are also called scratchings. Look for turkey **scat**, or droppings. This will tell you what the turkey that left them was eating. If you see berries, look for a berry patch. That will be a good place to hunt! Good turkey hunters know how to think like a turkey.

Good hunters do not only think like a turkey. They also trick turkeys. The most common way to trick a turkey is to use a turkey call. These can be the size and shape of whistles. They can also be noise-making boxes.

Turkeys make many different noises, so there are many different kinds of calls. Sometimes turkeys sound like they are purring. They do this when they are happy. Some calls sound like hens in order to attract gobblers. Other calls produce a noise that turkeys make when they are in danger. This might make a turkey raise its head or stop in its tracks. Turkeys are fooled only if the calls sound real. It is important to practice your call.

Did You Know?

When using a turkey call, you need to know what turkeys really sound like. Watch some videos of turkeys to become familiar with the noises they make.

This turkey hunter is using a box call. These calls are traditionally made out of wood.

15

Clever hunters also use decoys to fool birds. A decoy is a statue of a turkey. Good decoys look very real. A well-placed decoy can draw turkeys closer to the hunter. A decoy hen might draw a real gobbler that is hoping to mate. Decoys can be in the form of turkeys that are walking, strutting, or even feeding. A decoy of a feeding turkey might trick a hungry bird that is looking for food.

These hunters are being smart and putting their decoys in a bag to move them.

Placing your decoys well is a skill. Set them up in a spot that you will have a clear view of from your hunting spot.

Placing decoys can be dangerous. Make sure there are no other hunters in the area. Always keep your decoy in a bag while you carry it. If it can fool a turkey, it can also fool a hunter. You don't want someone shooting at your decoy while it is in your hands!

Did You Kno

Use a decoy in the open w turkeys might see it. Make there is enough room betv you and your decoy so tha have space to move arou

Along with turkeys, shotguns are used to hunt other birds, such as pheasants, quail, and ducks.

Most turkey hunters use shotguns. Unlike other firearms, shotguns do not shoot single bullets. They shoot shells filled with shot. Shot looks like tiny pellets. These pellets are packed inside the shell. A shotgun scatters the shot over a small area. This is why shotguns are sometimes called scatterguns. Shotguns are very powerful at close range, but they are not useful for faraway targets.

It is important to pick the right shotgun. Make sure that you can handle the weight and **recoil**. You must also think about your shotgun's **gauge**. Smaller numbers for the gauge actually mean bigger and more powerful shells. For example, a .12 gauge is bigger than a .20 gauge. Most beginners hunt turkeys with .20-gauge shotguns. These have more than enough power to bring down a turkey.

Left: *This hunter is opening a shotgun to reload it.* Bottom: *As shotguns do, shells come in several gauges.*

It is a good idea to practice shooting long before you go hunting. Try shooting at targets from different distances. This way you will know how well you can shoot and how close you will need to get. Make sure that you know your state's hunting and firearm laws.

Though turkey hunting takes place only in certain seasons, you can practice your shooting all year round.

Do not take your turkey decoy out of its bag until you are ready to place it.

Never forget that you have enough power in your hands to kill another human being. The most important rule is "know your target." You must be positive before you shoot. What if that sound is another hunter calling a turkey? What if what you see is a decoy being carried by a hunter in camouflage? Never try to sneak up on a turkey. Turkeys do not fall for this, and there is a good chance that a hunter is nearby waiting to shoot.

Shotguns are actually fairly new inventions. Other firearms have been around for a lot longer. One of these is the muzzleloader. You might have seen an old war movie in which the soldiers pour gunpowder down the barrels of their guns. They then load the barrels with bullets that are actually lead balls. They fire, and then they have to start the process all over again.

A muzzleloader produces a cloud of smoke when it is fired.

You can often see muzzleloaders at living-history museums and historical firearms demonstrations.

Muzzleloaders work much like this. You might think of them as small cannons.

Hunters that use muzzleloaders enjoy a challenge. Muzzleloader rifles and shotguns require excellent aim. Muzzleloader rifles do not scatter shot like shotguns. If you miss with a muzzleloader shotgun, it takes a long time to reload it. Your first shot has to count.

Bow hunters often use arrows called broadheads when hunting for turkeys.

Bow hunting provides its own challenges. It is important to pick the right bow. In the United States, the strength of a bowstring is measured in poundage. A bow hunter trying to shoot a deer at a far range will want more poundage than a turkey hunter at close range. A good starting point for beginners is 20 pounds.

It is important to remember that turkeys can see colors very clearly. It is a good idea to cover the **fletching** of your arrows with camouflage. Many hunters use a special net for this. Shotgun and muzzleloader hunters usually aim for a turkey's chest. Bow hunters who are expert shots can shoot turkeys in the neck or head. This kills a turkey quickly so that it does not feel much pain.

As you can see, a turkey's neck and head present a much smaller target than its chest does.

What should you do once you kill your turkey? Some hunters get them stuffed by **taxidermists** and turn their kills into art. Other hunters make necklaces from gobbler spurs. You can even use their feathers to make a fan.

Some turkey hunters compete by "scoring" their turkeys. A gobbler gets its score by adding its weight to its spur length and beard length. The hunter with the highest score wins.

June is National Turkey Lovers' Month. You are encouraged to eat a second Thanksgiving during the month of June to celebrate!

Most hunters decide to transform their turkeys into delicious meals. They believe that wild turkey tastes much better than turkey purchased in a store. There are many recipes for wild turkey on the Internet and in cookbooks. You can enjoy turkey any time. It does not have to be Thanksgiving!

Did You Know

Native Americans often ate wild turkey. However, people from some tribes, such as the Cheyenne and Apache, would not touch the bird.

A successful hunter will often pose for a photo with the turkey he just bagged.

Hunting wild turkey is a fun activity that everyone has the right to enjoy. However, we must all be careful. Wild turkeys almost became **extinct** in the 1920s and 1930s. Americans did not pay attention to the turkeys' habitat, and it started to vanish. Over the years, scientists and hunters worked side by side to bring the turkey back.

Many people hunt turkeys on public lands, such as state parks and wildlife refuges.

U.S.
RESERVATION
BOUNDARY
MARK
DO NOT
DISTURB

PUBLIC
HUNTING

Happily, turkeys have made a comeback. There are now more than seven million wild turkeys in North America.

Today, hunting laws protect wild turkeys. It might seem strange that hunters try to kill turkeys and also work hard to save them. However, many hunters think of themselves as **environmentalists**. They love hunting and they value animals. They do not want to see their way of life destroyed. Thanks to their hard work, wild turkeys will be around and enjoyed for a long time.

HUNTING TIPS

1 When calling a turkey, sit at the bottom of a large tree. You can be hidden and should be safe from other hunters.

2 Keep your calls low. If you are too loud, the turkey will expect you to come to it.

3 Scout out your location the day before, and mark places where you hear turkeys on a map.

4 Don't forget to wear dark or camouflage socks. This can help the turkey from spotting you when you sit down.

5 If a gobbler answers your call but won't come, try a different call or a new location.

6 Put the Sun to your back. The turkey will have a harder time seeing you because of the glare.

7 Turkeys do not like to climb or walk down hills. Get to their level.

8 If you arrive at your spot before sunrise, you are more likely to go unnoticed.

9 Act like your decoy. If a turkey looks your way, be perfectly still.

GLOSSARY

bag limit (BAG LIH-mut) How many of a certain kind of animal a hunter is allowed to kill.

camouflage (KA-muh-flahj) A color or a pattern that matches the surroundings and helps hide something.

environmentalists (in-vy-run-MEN-tuh-lusts) People who want to keep the natural world safe.

extinct (ik-STINGKT) No longer existing.

fletching (FLECH-ing) The things at the end of an arrow that steady its movement through the air when it is shot.

game birds (GAYM BURDZ) Birds that are hunted for sport.

gauge (GAYJ) A measure of how wide the barrel of a gun is.

habitat (HA-buh-tat) The kind of land where an animal or a plant naturally lives.

license (LY-suns) Official permission to do something.

recoil (REE-koy-ul) The push-back of a gun after it is fired.

roosts (ROOSTS) Places where animals rest or sleep.

scat (SKAT) Animal droppings.

subspecies (SUB-spee-sheez) Different kinds of the same animal.

taxidermists (TAK-suh-der-mists) People who prepare the bodies of animals that have died so that they can be shown.

INDEX

A
Americans, 4, 28

B
beard(s), 6–7, 26

C
call(s), 14, 30
camouflage, 11–12, 21, 25

D
decoy, 16–17, 21, 30

F
fletching, 25
Franklin, Benjamin, 4

G
gobbler(s), 6–8, 11, 14, 16, 26, 30

H
habitat, 12, 28
hen(s), 8, 14, 16

L
license, 9

M
muzzleloader(s), 22–23, 25

N
North America, 6

P
pellets, 18

R
roosts, 11–12

S
scat, 13
scatterguns, 18
scientists, 28
shotgun(s), 18–19, 22–23, 25
subspecies, 6

T
taxidermists, 26
Thanksgiving, 4, 27

WEBSITES

Due to the changing nature of Internet links, PowerKids Press has developed an online list of websites related to the subject of this book. This site is updated regularly. Please use this link to access the list:
www.powerkidslinks.com/lgh/turkey/